D1537701

Incredible
Reptiles

John Townsend

Chicago, Illinois

For information, address the publisher:
Raintree, 100 N. LaSalle, Suite 1200, Chicago, IL 60602
Customer Service: 888-363-4266
Visit our website at www.raintreelibrary.com

Printed and bound in China by South China Printing Company.
09 08 07 06 05
10 9 8 7 6 5 4 3 2 1

Library of Congress Cataloging-in-Publication Data

Townsend, John, 1955-
  Incredible reptiles / John Townsend.
    p. cm. -- (Incredible creatures)
  Summary: Looks at the behavior and characteristics of different reptiles, from the hard-shelled tortoises, turtles and terrapins to the geckos and skinks that can shed their tails and run when captured by a predator.
  Includes bibliographical references (p.   ) and index.
  ISBN 1-4109-0532-2 (Library Binding-hardcover) -- ISBN 1-4109-0856-9 (Paperback)
  1. Reptiles--Juvenile literature. [1. Reptiles.] I. Title. II. Series: Townsend, John, 1955-   Incredible creatures.
  QL644.2.T698 2004
  597.9--dc22
                                    2003020294

Acknowledgments
The publishers would like to thank the following for permission to reproduce photographs: p. 4 Kevin Schaffer/NHPA; pp. 4–5, 19, 20–21, 26 Minden Pictures/FLPA; pp. 5 (bottom), 23 (right), 32–33, 35, 37 (right), 38 (top) Anthony Bannister/NHPA; p. 5 (middle) John Shaw/NHPA; pp. 5 (top), 7, 9, 23 (left), 24 (left), 44–45, 45 Daniel Heuclin/NHPA; p. 6 Photodisc; pp. 6–7, 34 Lynn M. Stone/Nature Photo Library; p. 8 C. Carvalho/FLPA; pp. 8–9 Nigel J. Dennis/NHPA; p. 10 Theo Allofs/Corbis; p. 11 (left) Martin Harvey/NHPA; p. 11 (right) Digital Vision; pp. 12, 13 Derek Middleton/FLPA; pp. 12–13, 16–17, 24–25 Ant Photo Library/NHPA; p. 14 Brian Turner/FLPA; pp. 14–15 Earl Switak/NHPA; p. 15 E. Hanumantha Rao/NHPA; p. 16 George McCarthy/Corbis; pp. 17, 34–35 E & D Hosking/FLPA; pp. 18, 22, 36 Stephen Dalton/NHPA; pp. 18–19 James Warwick/NHPA; p. 20 Yossi Eshbol/Corbis; p. 21 Pete Atkinson/NHPA; pp. 25, 39 James Carmichael, Jr./NHPA; pp. 26–27 Martin Wendler/NHPA; p. 27 (right) Chris Mattison/FLPA; p. 28 (left) Rex Features; p. 29 (top) Winfried Wisniewski/FLPA; pp. 30, 33 Zig Leszczynski, Animals Animals/Oxford Scientific Films; pp. 30–31 Fred Bruemmer/Bruce Coleman Collection; p. 31 (top) Fritz Polking/FLPA; p. 32 Jany Sauvanet/NHPA; p. 38 (bottom) Dave Watts; p. 39 (bottom) S. C. Brown/FLPA; p. 40 Bruce Beehler/NHPA; pp. 40–41, 43 K. Ghani/NHPA; p. 41 (inset) Gondwana Studios; p. 42 Ferrero-Labat/Ardea; p. 44 Hanne & Jens Erickson/Nature Photo Library; p. 46 (left) David Middleton/NHPA; pp. 46–47 Nik Wheeler/Corbis; p. 47 Juan M. Renjifo/Oxford Scientific Films; p. 48 Neil Bowman/FLPA; p. 49 David A. Northcott/Corbis; p. 50 (left) Bill Ross/Corbis; pp. 50–51 Oxford Scientific Films; p. 51 (right) FLPA.

Cover photograph of a chameleon reproduced with permission of Frans Lanting, Minden Pictures/FLPA.

The publishers would like to thank Mark Rosenthal and Jon Pearce for their assistance in the preparation of this book.

Every effort has been made to contact copyright holders of any material reproduced in this book. Any omissions will be rectified in subsequent printings if notice is given to the publishers.

Disclaimer
All the Internet addresses (URLs) given in this book were valid at the time of going to press. However, due to the dynamic nature of the Internet, some addresses may have changed, or sites may have changed or ceased to exist since publication. While the author and publishers regret any inconvenience this may cause readers, no responsibility for any such changes can be accepted by either the author or the publishers.

The paper used to print this book comes from sustainable resources.

Contents

Any words appearing in the text in bold, **like this,** are explained in the glossary. You can also look out for them in the "Wild Words" bank at the bottom of each page.

The World of Reptiles

Four types of reptile

- Giant tortoises can live more than 150 years. Some of them alive today may have seen the scientist Charles Darwin in the 1850s. He went to their home on the Galapagos Islands to figure out how animals change and adapt.

- Crocodiles eat rocks!

- The longest snake can reach 36 ft (11 m).

- The tuatara (shown below) has hardly changed in 240 million years.

Reptiles have been on Earth for more than 250 million years. Scientists think that dinosaurs **evolved** from early reptiles. At one time they were probably the biggest animals ever to walk on Earth. Today, there are almost 6,000 kinds of reptiles. They all have some things in common.

Reptiles all have backbones, so they are **vertebrates.** They all breathe air with lungs. Their skin has **scales.** They are cold-blooded. This means they do not make their own body heat and depend on their surroundings to keep warm.

Most reptiles lay eggs, but some give birth to live young. Most reptiles have four legs, but some have two—or none!

amphibian   cold-blooded animal that lives in water and on land
evolve   develop and change over time

Reptile roots

Many scientists believe that **amphibians** crawled out of the water about 400 million years ago. They think some may have begun to lay eggs on land. In time, they evolved into reptiles with tougher skins and developed lungs. **Fossils** have been found of **ancient** reptiles of many shapes and sizes. *Dinosaur* means "terrible lizard."

Today, there are four main groups of reptiles. Each group includes some incredible animals.

- Turtles, tortoises, and terrapins form a group called **chelonians.**
- **Crocodilians** have four members: crocodiles, alligators, caimans, and gavials.
- Snakes and lizards belong to the same group.
- Tuataras are animals in their own group. They look like lizards, but they are not.

Find out later . . .

Which reptile can walk on water?

Which reptile eats the most people?

Which deadly snake is frighteningly fast?

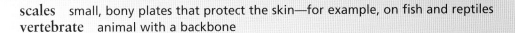

◀ The Galapagos tortoise lives on the Galapagos Islands, in the Pacific Ocean by South America.

scales   small, bony plates that protect the skin—for example, on fish and reptiles
vertebrate   animal with a backbone

Meet the Family

No slime

Reptiles are never slimy. Their scales often have a dry, silky feel to them. Some snakes have rougher skin, like sandpaper. Many water snakes, for example, have rough skin to help them wrap around **prey** and grip tightly under water.

One of the things that makes reptiles special is their skin, which is covered in **scales.** These scales may be small and overlapping, as in many lizards and snakes. Or they may be large and solid, as in turtles. Turtle scales are called **scutes.** The scales on the back of a large crocodile make tough armor that can even be bulletproof.

As lizards and snakes grow, their scales do not grow with them. Their old scales must be replaced by a larger set. That is why these reptiles **shed** their skin as they grow or when the old layer gets worn. A python will wriggle free of its old skin, which comes off inside out. Even its clear eyelids peel off—sort of like contact lenses.

bask   lie in the warmth of the sun
mammal   warm-blooded animal that has hair and feeds milk to its young

Chilly blood

Reptiles have to be warmed up by the sun before they are able to do anything. If it is too cold, their bodies cannot work very well. **Mammals** such as humans are different. We use some of the energy from our food to keep our bodies warm. We burn up much more energy this way. Because of this, mammals have to eat much more than reptiles.

Reptiles can still **survive** in the cold. It is just that their heart rates slow down and their bodies almost close down. A reptile **basking** in the sun soon raises its body temperature, and it is then ready to get going. It can easily overheat, so reptiles tend to hide in the shade when the sun beats down.

Lizard suntan

The rhinoceros iguana (shown below) changes color. Its scales are dark in the cool of the morning and evening. The dark color helps it absorb the sun's heat better. At midday, when the sun blazes down, the iguana's skin becomes lighter to reflect the heat and keep it cooler.

◀ A python's scaly skin regularly wears out and needs replacing.

prey   animal that is killed and eaten by other animals
scute   one of the tough, bony plates that make a tortoise shell

Natural heavyweight

The Aldabra tortoise (shown below) is one of the largest tortoises. The male's shell length can measure 4 ft (1.2 m) and it can weigh up to 550 lb (250 kg). Like the Galapagos tortoise, this large reptile can live to more than 150 years of age.

Shelled reptiles

There are about 250 **species** of tortoises, turtles, and terrapins. Hard shells protect their heads and feet when danger strikes. They simply hide inside.

The leopard tortoise is one of the largest mainland tortoises. Its yellowish shell with dark spots gives it its name. It can reach about 24 in. (60 cm) in length and weigh up to 70 lb (32 kg). Leopard tortoises live in the wild in Africa and can **survive** 75 years in **captivity.**

Some people think you can figure out the age of a tortoise by counting the rings on its shell. This is wrong. The rings form during growth periods, but these happen at different times and speeds throughout the year.

FAST FACTS

Weights for comparison
- 90 lb (40 kg)   a large dog
- 175 lb (80 kg)   an adult man
- 550 lb (250 kg)   a large lion
- 1,100 lb (500 kg)   a horse
- 2,000 lb (907 kg)   a small car

▲ A leopard tortoise moves across the Kalahari Desert.

algae   types of simple plant without stems that grow in water and on rocks
camouflage   color or pattern that matches the background

Turtles

There are about 200 species of freshwater turtle and seven types of sea turtle. The alligator snapping turtle is the largest freshwater turtle. It weighs 155 to 175 lb (70–80 kg). Males spend their whole lives in water, but females go on land to lay eggs. Like most reptiles, turtles do not interact with each other. They can stay underwater for up to 50 minutes at a time and then pop up for air. They stay very still underwater so that **algae** may cover their backs. This makes good **camouflage.**

Snapping turtles come from the southeastern region of the United States. There is a story that a 403-lb (183-kg) snapping turtle was found in the Neosho River in Kansas in 1937. Now that really would be a giant snapper!

Snapping turtle

The name of the snapping turtle (shown below) says it all. As it opens its jaws, it wiggles a wormlike flap to attract fish. Then it snaps. In Medina, Ohio, in 1999, a snapping turtle bit a nine-year-old boy in a stream. He was swimming when the turtle swam up and bit off his big toe.

FAST FACTS

The largest sea turtle is the leatherback. It can grow up to 8 ft (2.4 m) long and weigh over 1,750 lb (800 kg).

captivity   held in a cage or tank; the way animals are held in a zoo
species   type of animal or plant

Crocodilians

Crocodilians are very successful **predators** of rivers, lakes, swamps, and sometimes the sea. All 23 **species** have thick, scaly armor, from crocodiles and alligators to caimans and gavials. The smallest is the dwarf caiman at 5 ft (1.5 m) long. The biggest is the saltwater crocodile. It can grow to almost 20 ft (6 m) in length. Nile crocodiles can also be giants at almost 20 ft (6 m). These crocodiles can live for 40 years in the wild and twice that in zoos.

The main difference between crocodiles and alligators is the shape of their snout. The crocodile has more of a pointed V-shaped nose. It also has two teeth sticking up from its bottom jaw when it closes its mouth. Crocodiles live across the southern part of the world, but alligators only live in the Americas and China.

Caimans

Caimans are like small alligators, although the black caiman of South America can grow to over 13 ft (4 m) long.

▼ Caimans have short snouts and bony ridges around their eye sockets.

crocodilian   reptiles such as crocodiles, alligators, caimans, and gavials
endangered   at risk of disappearing forever

Alligators

American alligators can grow to over 13 ft (4 m). One caught in the United States was reported to be 19 ft (5.8 m) long. There could be more than a million alligators in the swamps of Florida. Alligators feed on fish and can even leap from the swamp to catch the occasional bird. Attacks by alligators on humans are very rare.

The Chinese alligator lives where the winters are very cold. Slowly the rivers freeze over, so the alligator has to keep the tip of its nose poking above the ice. This is how it breathes while its body "closes down" for the winter and waits for the **thaw**. Only when its blood warms up again can it become active.

Gavials

These reptiles, like the one shown below, are sometimes called gharials. They have long, narrow snouts with lumps on the ends. This shape is good for catching fish. In Hindi they call them *ghara*, which means "a pot." They come from Southeast Asia and are now an **endangered** species.

► A female Nile crocodile guards her nest.

predator　animal that hunts and eats other animals
thaw　when ice or snow melts

Long body, short legs

The common lizard (below) lives across Europe and northern Asia. As its name suggests, it is the most common lizard in northern areas like the United Kingdom. In fact, this lizard is the only reptile found in Ireland. It is usually 4 to 6 in. (10–16 cm) long.

Lizards

There are more than 3,700 different kinds of lizard. There may also be more we do not yet know about. About one-third of all lizards are skinks. These are lizards with short legs or no legs at all. As such, they tend to live on the ground and often burrow into the earth. The Florida sand skink has very short legs that it uses to crawl. When it is in a hurry, it lifts its legs out of the way and moves its body from side to side like a snake.

The blue-tongued skink of Australia grows to 18 in. (45 cm) long. It crawls through the **scrub** eating small animals and berries. Not many animals can brag about having a long, blue tongue!

FAST FACTS

- The biggest lizard is the Komodo dragon, at almost 10 ft (3 m) long.
- The water monitor is nearly 10 ft (3 m) long.
- The perenty lizard (see page 25) can be more than 8 ft (2.5 m) long.

forked tongue   long tongue that divides into two at the tip

Bigger lizards

Monitor lizards have a strong body. They have long legs and a long neck. They are the only lizards to have a thin **forked tongue,** just like a snake's. They can move fast and hunt over long distances. They can also stand up on their rear legs to get a good view.

Although not as big as the Komodo dragon, the Salvadori's monitor lizard is the longest lizard. With its very long tail, it can reach almost 10 ft (3 m) long. It spends much of its time in the trees of New Guinea. Its black-and-white skin is used by native people for making drums. It is sometimes called the crocodile monitor. Although it is not usually aggressive, it can give quite a swipe with its long, strong tail.

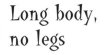

Long body, no legs

Slowworms look like snakes or skinks, but they are really legless lizards. Unlike snakes, most lizards and slowworms have eyelids. There are about 100 kinds of slowworm. One of the United States' rarest legless lizards is the size of a pencil. The black legless lizard lives only in Monterrey County, California. Only one is found in the United Kingdom, mostly in Wales and the southwest of England.

◄ A blue-tongued skink shows off its tongue.

scrub   area of thorny bushes and tufts of grass

- Adders (vipers) like
  the one below
  are the most widely
  found snake in
  northern areas.
  They are the only
  species of snake
  found inside the
  Arctic Circle. The
  adder is also the
  United Kingdom's
  only poisonous reptile.

- There are twenty
  different poisonous
  snakes in the United
  States. All states have
  at least one of them,
  apart from Maine,
  Alaska, and Hawaii.

- A news story in
  2004 told of a
  python found in
  Indonesia. It was said to
  be almost 50 ft (15 m)
  long and weigh
  100 lb (450 kg).

Snakes

There are nearly 2,400 **species** of snakes. Some
are a few inches long and others are
several feet. Some slither along the ground,
some swim, and others climb trees and "fly."
The flying snake of Java can flatten itself like a
ribbon and sail like a glider from tree to tree.

The fastest land snake is the black mamba of
Africa. It can keep up a speed of 7 mi (11 km) per
hour over 150 ft (46 m) or sprint for short bursts
at 15 mi (24 km) per hour.

The sidewinder desert rattlesnake of North
America moves sideways over loose sand.
Because the sand is so hot, only small parts
of its body touch the ground at any one time.
It lifts its middle right side off the ground and
leaves behind a tell-tale pattern in the desert.

▲ A sidewinder leaves
its trail across Death
Valley, California.

14   Wild Words   reticulated   having a pattern of lines and squares; looking like a net
venom   poison

For the record

The world's longest recorded snake is the **reticulated** python, which can reach a length of 35 ft (10.7 m). There have been reports of even longer snakes of 98 ft (30 m), but none has been proved.

Giant anacondas have sometimes reached 33 ft (10 m) and are much heavier than reticulated pythons. These snakes are not often seen, since they spend a lot of time sleeping off a large kill. On occasion they have died by swallowing large **prey** with horns that stab their insides after being swallowed.

As long as they are not too greedy, some large snakes can live for a long time. The longest-living snake on record was a 44-year-old African ball python.

Some other long snake records

Indian python diamond:
24.9 ft (7.6 m)
Python:
21 ft (6.4 m)
King cobra:
19 ft (5.8 m)
Boa constrictor:
16.1 ft (4.9 m)
Bushmaster:
12.1 ft (3.7 m)
Giant brown snake:
11.2 ft (3.7 m)

JUST TO HELP COMPARE . . .

Most family cars are about 10 to 13 ft (3–4 m) long from front bumper to back bumper.

▶ King cobras are the world's longest **venomous** snakes.

Under threat

Tuataras once lived in many parts of the world, but now only a few **survive** on small islands off New Zealand. They had very few predators until humans came to New Zealand with dogs and rats. Today, tuataras are only found on islands without rats.

▼ Rats compete with tuataras for food.

Tuataras

The tuatara of New Zealand may look like any other lizard. However, scientists have found that it is different from other reptiles. It has an extra bone in its skull, and its teeth are part of its jawbone.

The tuatara is like a lizard in some ways. It can **shed** its tail and grow it again. In fact, the males often lose their tails in fights during the **breeding** season. Male tuataras have a **crest** of spikes all down their backs. Females lay eggs that take fifteen months to hatch. That is much longer than any other reptile.

crest   line along the head, neck, and back of some animals
environment   natural surroundings

On guard

Adult tuataras are mainly **nocturnal**. It is safer that way, sincethey can avoid **predators**. Tuataras live in burrows. They can dig their own, but they often use those left by other animals and birds. They sometimes come to the entrance of their burrows to **bask** in the sun, but they prefer to keep out of the way. Unlike most reptiles, they can stay active when they get cold.

Young tuataras are more active in the daytime. This is because they need to avoid the adults, who sometimes try to eat them. Tuataras are mostly sit-and-wait predators. They stay still and then grab **prey** that comes near, such as young birds and lizards . . . or even their own young.

Old age

Tuataras on the cooler islands, like the one below, grow more slowly than those in warmer **environments**. Very little is known about these tuataras— but it is thought they might live for up to 120 years.

◀ A male tuatara can grow to 24 in. (60 cm) long.

nocturnal   active at night and not in the day
shed   get rid of or lose

Amazing Bodies

Lung power

A snake's long, thin body does not have much room for a pair of lungs, so its left lung is much smaller than the right, or even missing. It can still breathe perfectly well. Snakes such as the grass snake below prefer to swim in shallow water so that they can come up for air.

All reptiles breathe through lungs, which means they are suited to life on land. But they cannot breathe underwater.

Breathing

Sea turtles and sea snakes are the only reptiles that spend nearly all of their lives in water. These reptiles need more than just lungs to help them breathe, since they spend so long underwater. Sea turtles are able to take some **oxygen** from the water through the insides of their mouths. Some sea snakes can do the same through their skin.

Unlike amphibians, all young reptiles have lungs. None begins life with **gills** for breathing. They gulp in air through their mouths as soon as they come into the world.

▲ A spectacled caiman surfaces in a Brazilian river.

gills   organs that some animals have to breathe underwater
carbon dioxide   gas that animals breathe out

Deep breaths

Crocodilians spend a lot of time underwater. They breathe through their nostrils, which poke above the water's surface. They are able to hold their breath for up to an hour when they dive. Crocodilians do not have lips, so they are unable to seal their mouths underwater. Instead, they have two flaps at the back of their throat to stop water from gushing down their mouths and filling their lungs. This allows crocodiles and alligators to open their mouths underwater to eat **prey** without the risk of drowning.

Unlike other reptiles, crocodilians have a heart with four chambers. This keeps their blood pumping through the lungs to collect oxygen and to get rid of **carbon dioxide.**

▼ Salt water crocodiles can swim long distances underwater.

Under water

In a crocodile's heart, two chambers pump blood to and from the lungs. Two other chambers pump blood around the rest of the body. When a crocodile dives, it can open **valves** in the heart to stop blood from going into the lungs, which do not work underwater. The blood goes to the crocodile's hard-working muscles.

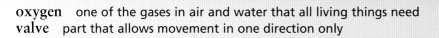

oxygen   one of the gases in air and water that all living things need
valve   part that allows movement in one direction only

19

Turtle power

Sea turtles live almost entirely in water. Females can stay out of water for a few hours when they come ashore to lay eggs. If they get hot or cannot get back to the water, they will die.

To sleep, turtles may dive to the seabed and jam themselves under a rock. They do not breathe while they sleep, but every hour or so they wake up and swim to the surface to get air. Then they go back down to sleep some more. Turtles that live in very deep water sleep at the surface with their nostrils poking out of the water.

Large leatherback turtles can dive to almost 1 mi (1.6 km) deep for about an hour. That requires an amazing body!

Terrapins

Terrapins, like the one below, are often called diamondbacks because of the diamond-shaped rings on their shells. They are the only turtles in the world that live in **brackish** water. The word *terrapin* comes from an Indian word meaning "a little turtle." Terrapins always live near water.

▶ A marine iguana dives to graze on the seabed.

brackish   slightly salty
herbivore   animal that only eats plants

Lizards underwater

Even though reptiles have to keep breathing air, some **species** spend a lot of time in or underwater. A few live in the sea all the time. Sea turtles, a **marine** iguana, and more than 70 species of snakes live in the sea.

With their short, stubby legs, lizards do not make the best swimmers. Yet the marine iguana of the Galapagos Islands is the world's only sea lizard. It uses its tail as a paddle to go swimming for food. It returns to land to **bask** in the sun to warm up. Marine iguanas are **herbivores** and eat seaweed. They generally dive for only a few minutes, but there are records of iguanas staying under the sea for 45 minutes.

Snakes of the sea

Snakes like the banded sea snake below can swim to depths of 150 ft (45 m), where they feed on fish, eels, and crabs. They need to swim to the surface to get air about every two hours. However, some can stay below water for up to eight hours.

marine   to do with the sea

Feeding

Busy insect-eaters

Although most lizards are tropical, some live in cold **climates** 16,400 ft (5,000 m) high in the mountains. Many are important in controlling insects. Some lizards eat half their weight in insects in one night.

Most reptiles are **carnivores,** which means they eat other animals. Very few are **herbivores** and eat only plants. Many are **insectivores** and eat mainly insects. Some are **omnivores,** meaning they eat a mixture of both animals and plants.

Finding food

Unlike many birds and **mammals,** reptiles do not have to spend most of their time looking for food. They spend most of their time **digesting** it, so they may go days or weeks without eating.

Most tortoises are herbivores, although some eat insects and snails. Some reptiles, such as crocodiles, are skilled killers of large **prey.** There is one thing crocodiles eat that is not meat: rocks! They swallow these to grind up the heavy food inside their **gizzards.** The rocks also weigh them down and keep them underwater.

FAST FACTS

Birds, like reptiles, also have gizzards. Some swallow tiny pebbles to help grind up their food.

◄ A chameleon's tongue is as long as its body, with a sticky tip for catching insects.

climate   general weather conditions in an area over a period of time
digest   break down food in the body

Hunting

So how do reptiles find their food? They either go out looking for it or they lie in wait and let it come to them. Many reptiles are masters of **ambush. Crocodilians** and large snakes can hide underwater until prey comes along for a drink. They then strike with amazing speed and power.

Other snakes just quietly slither around or hang from a branch. They are always on the lookout—with their tongues. They keep flicking their tongues to "taste" the air. In addition to smelling prey like this, some snakes can also sense the body heat of their victims. Many snakes swallow prey that is up to three times wider than their own body. It is just a matter of stretching. Snakes are the world's most effective natural control of **rodents.**

Croc teeth

Crocodilians grow hundreds of teeth during their lives. They need them for gripping and gulping, since they cannot chew their food. Their teeth often fall out, but it does not matter, since new ones grow to replace them.

◄ This green rat snake is tasting the air.

gizzard   part of a bird's or reptile's stomach that grinds down food
rodent   small mammal with teeth, such as rats, mice, and squirrels

Crush and gulp

Most lizards have pointed teeth that are all alike. They do not have special teeth for grinding, so they cannot chew up food very well. Instead, they crush it in their mouths and then they gulp it down whole.

Eating

Reptiles rely on their teeth. Only turtles and tortoises do not have any. They bite with the sharp, bony edges of their mouths instead. Just about every **species** of snake on Earth has teeth, but they are not used for chewing. Snakes eat their **prey** whole. Their teeth are used for holding onto the prey to stop it from escaping. Some snakes have **venom** in two fangs. The venom may stun or kill their prey, but it has another use. It helps the snakes **digest** their food. Venom helps to break down the meat as it goes through a snake's body.

Anacondas have teeth, but they are not **venomous** snakes. They rely on their enormous size and power to kill their victims. It is possible to be bitten by an anaconda, but the bite would not be **fatal.**

▲ Juicy insects are often on the green lizard's menu.

fatal   causing death

The perenty

The perenty is the largest Australian monitor lizard, growing to more than 8 ft (2.5 m) long. It catches snakes, lizards, birds, and small **mammals.** It has even been known to catch small kangaroos. Those on Barrow Island eat baby turtles as they hatch and crawl to the sea. Perenties also eat the eggs of reptiles and birds. They even eat young perenties.

Slow digestion

Depending on the size of its meal, it can take from 60 seconds to two hours for a snake to eat its catch. Digestion of food may take up to two weeks. The average is from four to six days. It can take awhile for a lump of food to pass down the snake. Muscles squeeze it along. The same happens in our throats.

Matamata

The matamata turtle (shown below) from the Amazon River in South America has a strange arrow-shaped head. It uses the "gape and suck" way of eating. It lies in wait for a fish to come by, then suddenly opens its mouth wide. This sudden opening sucks in the fish like a vacuum cleaner.

◄ A perenty waits for a rabbit to come out of its burrow.

Saving water

Herbivore lizards such as the green iguana, below, get much of their moisture from plants. They make this water last by getting rid of salt from their bloodstreams. They do this through a salt **glands** on their noses. That is why they often sneeze out a crusty, white substance.

Digestion

Since reptiles are cold-blooded, the air temperature affects how well they **digest** their food. Below 71.6 °F (22 °C), crocodiles tend not to eat at all, since their digestive system slows down. If a snake is too cool after feeding, digestion cannot take place. There is not enough energy for its system to work. So there is only one thing for it. The snake throws it all up again. The food must come out again or it will rot inside the snake and kill it.

Some large snakes may feed less than six times a year. In fact, some have been known to starve for more than twelve months without any bad effects.

► Anacondas can kill a caiman, swallow it whole, and digest its tough body.

acid   liquid that can be strong enough to break down materials
gland   part of the body that makes hormones and other substances

Big appetites

Large snakes and **crocodilians** have strong **acids** in their stomachs. They need these acids to dissolve bones, skin, and feet of big **prey**. It takes a very strong stomach to break down an entire buffalo!

Anacondas are members of the boa constrictor family of snakes. This means that they kill their prey by coiling their long bodies around their **victims**. Then they grip and squeeze until their prey **suffocates**.

The snake then unhinges its jaw and swallows the victim whole. Although they are big and strong enough to eat people, anacondas do not do this often. They have been known to eat caimans, other snakes, deer, and even jaguars.

GIRL FIGHTS PYTHON TO SAVE KITTEN

Queensland, Australia, March 2003

A six-year-old girl won a special award for saving her kitten from a python. Marlie Coleman saw the python's jaws clamped around her kitten, Sooty, in her own backyard in the town of Cairns. She quickly grabbed her pet and tugged it from the fangs. The snake let go just in time.

▼ The Australian amethystine python will only attack small prey.

suffocate   choke or die from being unable to breathe
victim   animal that gets hurt or killed

CROC SNACKS ON STEVE IRWIN'S LEG

2001

The TV crocodile hunter Steve Irwin almost became a snack for a crocodile when a 6.6-ft (2-m) reptile sank its teeth into his leg. A 13-year-old female saltwater crocodile bit Irwin as he tried to move her into another pen at his Australian zoo. "This poor little female was just defending herself," he said. Irwin needed twelve stitches, but said it was "just part of the job!"

Predators and prey

Many small reptiles are low down the **food chain.** That means they are **prey** to larger **predators.** Large reptiles, however, are at the top of the food chain. Apart from humans, they do not to fear any other animals.

Salties

The saltwater crocodile is the biggest reptile on Earth. Saltwater crocodiles can live in the sea, often hundreds of miles from shore. But they are just as at home in rivers and lakes, where they snap up any creature in sight. Some of the biggest "salties" can weigh more than a ton. They kill more people than any other reptile. People who go hiking or swimming in the swamps of Australia and Asia are not always careful and are killed by crocodiles. Even so, more people die from bee stings each year than from crocodile attacks!

food chain   order in which one living thing feeds on another

Alligator attack

The **habitat** of alligators is often under threat, so they are forced into trouble.

In 1999 in Rio de Janeiro, Brazil, builders scared a 6.6-ft (2-m) long alligator out of its natural feeding grounds. The hungry reptile walked into a backyard and gulped down the owner's dog along with four chickens. It took four policemen 30 minutes to calm the alligator. At last they got it onto a stretcher and sent it safely to a zoo. "The city is spreading into the habitat of the alligators," the zoo's supervisor said. "They end up leaving the swamp because of noise or the lack of food. You cannot blame them."

Big eaters

Nile crocodiles live all over Africa and not just in the Nile River. Some are big enough to kill and eat zebras, buffalo, or even lions. Some have even been known to chase the occasional hippo or elephant.

◀ An American alligator opens wide.

habitat   natural home of an animal or plant

Breeding

Most of the time, reptiles do not have much to do with each other. Yet they will try all sorts of ways to find and impress a mate.

Did you know . . . ?

- The **marine** iguana normally has dark skin. During the mating season, it comes out in red spots. That is a signal to say, "I am ready to mate."

Meeting and mating

Male lizards often fight during the **breeding** season. The fighting is just for show but, even so, some get hurt.

Some geckos chirp and bark to attract a partner. Others bob up and down for hours.

The male common agama lizard threatens a rival by bobbing his head. Then he rears up on his back legs while his body turns pale and spotted. Males lash out at each other with their tails until one of them gives up.

The male eastern fence lizard shows off the bright blue skin on his throat. If the female is not ready to **mate,** she simply leaps away and ignores him.

FAST FACTS

Geckos are nocturnal lizards. Today geckos are kept as pets because they keep houses free of cockroaches. Although they have a fierce bite, they are thought to bring good luck in Hawaii.

Smelling good

Snakes attract each other by giving off scent through their skin. When a female adder is ready to breed, she leaves a scent as she slides through the grass. The male adder senses this with his tongue and is soon on her trail.

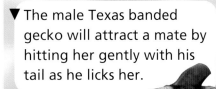

▼ The male Texas banded gecko will attract a mate by hitting her gently with his tail as he licks her.

hibernate   "close down" the body and rest when it is too cold or dry

Giving birth

Most snakes lay eggs, but some give birth to live young. Common garter snakes are found across North America. They **hibernate** for the winter in holes, where they all become a twisted, squirming mass. When they wake in the spring, hundreds of males wriggle over the twisting coils of females. They break up once they finish mating. The females do not lay eggs, but up to 60 young grow inside their body. The baby snakes are born two to three months later.

The anaconda is another snake that gives birth to live young rather than laying eggs.

Perfect partners

The male Nile crocodile calls a female by thrashing his tail through the water. The pair swims around in circles before mating. Alligators also mate in water, often at night. The male attracts a female by opening his jaws and roaring, as shown above. He gives off a scent from **glands** in his throat.

◄ Red-sided garter snakes come out from hibernation in a mass in the spring.

mate   when a female and male animal come together to produce young

Eggs, young, and parents

Reptile eggs can be leathery or have hard shells like a bird's egg. Geckos lay hard-shelled eggs that often stick to leaves or bark. Sometimes these get blown out to sea. As a result, geckos are found on many islands that other lizards have not reached.

Tortoises lay their eggs in soil. The young hatch and have to look after themselves. Rats and pigs often eat them, so it is not easy being a baby tortoise.

Most sea turtles return to the same beach where they hatched. Here, the female can lay 100 eggs, but very few young **survive** the race back to the sea. Birds, crabs, and fish are waiting to catch them. About only one percent of baby sea turtles live to become adults.

▼ Newly hatched loggerhead turtles head for the sea.

aggressive   hostile, angry, and bad-tempered
cannibal   animal that eats its own kind

Crocodile parents

Not many reptiles are known to be caring parents. They tend to leave their young to manage on their own. However, female **crocodilians** do look after their young. They guard them for weeks. Even other adults will answer the **distress call** of the young, which have many **predators.** A female alligator can be **aggressive** when she guards her nest from such predators as hungry raccoons. Fish, birds, and other reptiles are on the lookout for food, so the mother will sometimes carry her young in her mouth. Even so, only about two percent of crocodilian eggs survive to become adults.

In some **species,** the father stays nearby to guard the young. Yet if food gets short, he may turn into a **cannibal** and eat a few.

Breaking out

Like many young birds, some baby reptiles have an egg tooth. This is a sharp tooth on the upper lip, which the baby uses to cut itself out of the egg. The tooth drops off soon after the reptile has hatched.

▼ This baby sea turtle is hatching from its egg.

Defense

Fangs

Vipers, including adders and rattlesnakes like the eastern diamondback below, have large fangs that fold away in the roof of the snake's mouth. A flap of skin covers them until the snake needs them. Then the fangs spring forward to strike. Venom squirts down a **duct,** and the fangs are like needles injecting poison. Australia's brown snakes and tiger snakes have some of the deadliest fangs and venom.

Many reptiles have to defend themselves against **predators.** Snakes can scare off many animals just by looking like a snake!

Venom

Less than one-third of the world's snake **species** are poisonous, but in Australia, 65 percent of snakes have **venom.** Even so, only a few people die from snakebites in Australia in a year.

Less than 10 percent of snakes are dangerous to humans. In India, snakes kill people who walk around the countryside in bare feet. An Indian cobra can also spit its venom into someone's eyes, which causes blindness for a while.

The king cobra is bigger but less **toxic** than the Indian cobra. Even so, it can inject 0.014 oz (400 mg) of venom in a single bite. That is enough to kill ten adult humans or even an elephant.

▼ A gila monster's bright colors are a warning to predators.

diabetes   disease in which sugar is not correctly absorbed into the blood
duct   channel or tube for carrying fluid

Deadly lizard

The gila monster is one of only two species of lizards with venom. The Mexican beaded lizard is the other.

The gila bites and grips onto its **prey** with its teeth. It does not inject venom through fangs, like snakes. It has grooved teeth in its lower jaw. When it bites, the strong jaws chew the venom in through the grooves. Only a small amount of venom is given like this, so it is not usually deadly to humans.

Scientists are studying an extract from the gila monster's venom. They hope to use it in a new drug to treat a type of **diabetes.** It is still being tested, but there are signs it may help some patients.

Lethal snakes

- The Australian inland taipan releases just 0.004 oz (100 mg) of venom in one bite—enough to kill 100 people or 250,000 mice.
- The black mamba (shown below) can grow as long as 14 ft (4.3 m). It is fast and is one of the deadliest snakes of all. It can deliver enough venom to kill 260 people in one bite.

toxic   poisonous

Keeping still

As a chameleon clings onto a branch with its **prehensile** tail, only its eyes move. It does not have to move its body at all, since its eyes can swivel and see in two directions at once. Its tongue can be as long as its own body.

▼ A veiled chameleon is well camouflaged among the green leaves of its habitat.

Camouflage

There are 135 different chameleon **species,** which come from tropical Africa and India. Chameleons range in size from a few inches long to a type of chameleon called oustaleti that is over a foot and a half long. The amazing thing about chameleons is that they can change color. They seem able to blend in with all kinds of backgrounds. Their mood and temperature also affect their color.

This **camouflage** helps to defend the chameleon from **predators,** but it also lets it creep up on insects. One flick of its long sticky tongue and dinner is served. The tongue can dart out in less than a sixteenth of a second. This reptile spends its life waiting and watching . . .

prehensile   able to grip tightly, like a hand

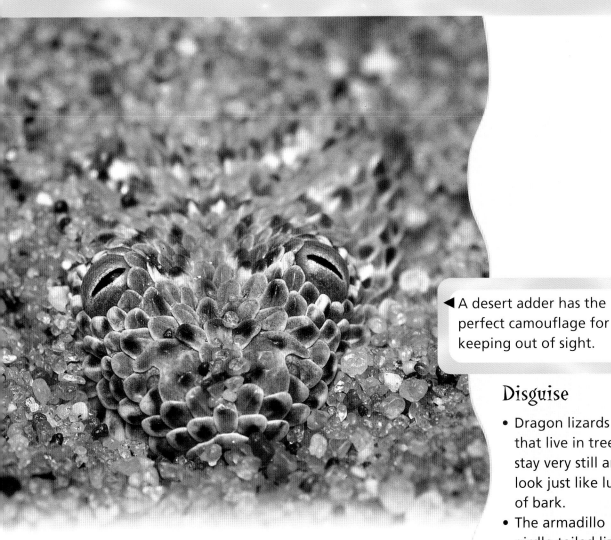

Disguise

- Dragon lizards that live in trees stay very still and look just like lumps of bark.
- The armadillo girdle-tailed lizard (shown below) curls up when it panics. Not only does it look like a pile of leaves, but it also protects itself with prickly armor.

Looks can save lives

Many forest snakes are green, brown, or spotted, so they blend in with the undergrowth. Others can stay completely still. Any predator will look for movement or color. Many other reptiles hunt snakes. Birds with very good eyesight are always on the lookout for a snake in the grass or the sand.

That is where the desert adder is very smart. It buries itself in sand so that only the top of its head sticks out. Since it is the color of sand, there is nothing to see. Even a sharp-eyed eagle would think the snake is just a rock.

Red and orange on a snake is a warning. It says "poison." But the false coral snake is not poisonous at all. Its bright colors just fool predators into thinking that it is deadly.

Causing a stink

The freshwater **musk** turtle (above) has another name: stinkpot. It lets out a foul-smelling liquid from its musk **glands.** Any predator will back away and leave the stinkpot in peace.

Special tricks

Reptiles have developed many ways to protect themselves. After all, there is always something nearby wanting a quick meal. To avoid being eaten, the Australian frilled lizard tries to look scary. It is all for show, since it cannot really do much harm. It opens its mouth, bares its teeth, waves a red tongue, hisses, and puffs out a frill around its neck. That is enough to scare almost all **predators.**

The green anole lizard scares attackers by puffing out a throat pouch. It has patches of bright red and blue skin. Males of other anole lizards raise **crests** on the backs of their necks and **inflate** throat pouches while making loud noises. It means just one thing: "Keep away!"

▲ A frilled lizard flares up to scare off predators.

hypnotize   put someone into a trance
inflate   blow up and enlarge

A great actor

The West Indian wood snake is a great actor. If it is threatened, it pretends to be dead and makes a smell like rotting flesh. If the predator will not give up, the snake fills its eyes with blood. For its final act, it bursts blood vessels in its mouth. So now it appears to be dead, stinks badly, looks like it is diseased, and bleeds from the mouth. That will surely turn an attacker off. The snake then escapes alive and well.

Keep off!

Cobras try various tricks to defend themselves. They can puff out their necks to look bigger, while some stare into an enemy's eyes. This seems to **hypnotize** some animals.

Rattlesnakes just shake their tails. The noise of their rattle warns everyone to keep their distance.

Bloodshot eyes

The Texas horned lizard has the greatest trick of all. When under threat, it bursts blood vessels in and around its eyes. It squirts a stream of blood into the face of an attacker. This shocks the predator so much that the tiny horned lizard has time to run away.

◄ The Texas horned lizard is only about 6 in. (15 cm) from snout to tail, so it needs a few tricks to scare predators off.

musk strong-smelling substance

Weird and Wonderful

Komodo dragons are huge lizards. Until 1912 no one knew about them. Some are almost 10 ft (3 m) long and weigh 330 lb (150 kg), but there have been reports of bigger ones.

These reptiles are **scavengers** and eat rotting flesh. They rely on their sense of smell to track down **carrion.** They kill for themselves, too, and can run as fast as a person. In fact, they have been known to kill humans. Their bite is deadly due to at least seven types of dangerous **bacteria** in their mouth. This is from **saliva** as well as rotting food stuck between the teeth. When they bite, the **victim** gets blood poisoning and quickly becomes sick. Then the dragons come in for the kill.

Fact or fiction?

Some people think a huge lizard bigger than a Komodo dragon may exist. It appears in stories from Papua New Guinea. Local people tell of a reptile 30 ft (9 m) long that hides in trees and drops on its prey. Soldiers in New Guinea during World War II reported reptiles of such a size.

▼ Giant lizards may live in the New Guinea rain forest.

bacteria   group of very tiny creatures that can cause disease
carrion   dead and rotting flesh

Eating habits

The Komodo dragon is the only reptile, apart from a turtle, that rips up its **prey** before it swallows chunks whole. In one meal it can eat nearly its own weight in meat. A dragon has been seen eating a whole pig in seventeen minutes. That is like someone eating 600 hamburgers at once! The Komodo dragon has a huge **gall bladder** to help it digest such large amounts.

KOMODO DRAGON ATTACKS BRONSTEIN

June 2001

Phil Bronstein, husband of actress Sharon Stone, is stable after surgery to join cut tendons in his foot. His big toe was crushed by a Komodo dragon's jaws. Bronstein and a zookeeper had just gone in the cage when the reptile attacked.

Big brother?

A huge lizard once lived in Australia. It was like a giant Komodo dragon and was called *Megalania*. Its skull (shown below) was more than 31 in. (80 cm) long. Some people think there could still be a few hidden in the swamps and forests. Now and then people report seeing such an animal.

gall bladder   organ of the body that stores bile and acid to help break down food
scavenger animal that feeds off scraps and the food of others

Super croc

Seventy million years ago, huge crocodiles walked on Earth. They were the size of a bus and probably hunted dinosaurs. Their huge **fossils** have been found in the Sahara Desert. They may also have lived in the swamps of what is now Texas.

Amazing crocodiles

Crocodiles have always amazed us. The ancient Egyptians saw them as gods. There is something about these creatures from a past age that makes us wonder: How have they survived for so long? It could be in their blood.

One of the strange things about crocodiles is that they tend to heal very fast if they get hurt. Crocodiles often get into fights and sometimes get their legs and tails torn off. Even if they get ripped open, their bodies soon repair. Other animals would die from such wounds. Scientists think there may be something special about crocodile blood. It seems to kill deadly **germs,** so perhaps it might be used in human medicine in the future.

▶ The Nile crocodile has vicious teeth, but one type of bird can go in its mouth safely.

fossil very old remains of things that once lived, found in rock and mud
germ very tiny living thing that causes disease

Best of friends

Most animals are very scared of crocodiles. They know to keep far away from the crocodile's powerful jaws, which can slam shut with great force. Yet one animal does not seem to care. In fact, it steps right into the gaping jaws.

Nile crocodiles often sunbathe with their mouths wide open. They let the breeze blow in their throats to keep them cool. But along comes a small wading bird called a crocodile bird—and in it hops! This bird picks the crocodile's teeth and gums clean of **parasites** or bits of meat. It gets a free dinner while the crocodile gets a free dentist. The bird just hops away again, and the crocodile never seems to snap.

▼ The marsh crocodile is also known as a mugger, from a Hindi word meaning "water monster."

parasite   animal or plant that lives in or on another living thing

Great escapes

Many lizards such as geckos and skinks have a great trick for getting away from anything that grabs hold of them. They simply **shed** their tail and run. They leave a twitching tail behind. That is enough to confuse any **predator.** The lizard loses very little blood, and it grows a new tail in just a few months. After all, its tail is important for balance and movement, so it would feel lost without it.

The new "bones" that grow are really tough **tissue** that soon builds up at the stump. The new **scales** that grow may look different from the rest of the lizard's body. But it is still a new tail, and it is soon ready for the next escape.

Mini reptile

A reptile can easily escape and hide if it is tiny. The Virgin Island gecko (shown below) is just under 1 in. (2 cm) when it is fully grown. That makes it one of the smallest lizards around. It can escape into the smallest of cracks.

tissue   soft parts of the body; a collection of cells

Running like magic

Another useful trick to get away fast is to run across the ceiling. The gecko lizard can run up glass or upside down on ceilings without falling. It has special pads of skin and tiny hairs on its toes that act like suction cups. These, along with claws that cling to surface bumps, help geckos climb any surface.

The basilisk lizard is an iguana from South America. It can run away on two legs. It can also run on water. Its secret is in its feet, which trap air pockets. It is like having balloons under each foot that stop it from sinking. Instead of running on water, it is really running on air. If the basilisk stopped, it would sink—but it can clear 130 ft (40 m) across a pond.

Zebra tail

A zebra-tailed lizard (below) has a black-and-white pattern under its tail. It waves this at any predator to put it into a **trance**. While the predator feels dazed, the lizard hops off quickly and escapes.

▼ Basilisk lizards are also called "Jesus lizards" after the story of Christ walking on water.

trance   in a sleeplike state

On the move

Reptiles are great survivors. They live in the hottest places, and some cope with severe cold. They **thrive** in water, swamps, or on dry land. Sometimes they have to **survive** in unusual places when people are cruel or careless. Pet reptiles are sometimes released or they escape into new surroundings.

The Everglades National Park in Florida has a problem with these pets in the wild. The state of Florida estimates that more than 1,000 snakes escaped into the wild after Hurricane Andrew in 1992. Even before then, people saw huge pythons from Asia living in Florida's swamps.

No one has found python eggs in Florida yet, but experts think they have begun **breeding** in the wild. Pythons could pose a serious threat to the wildlife of the Everglades.

Amazing travels

Some turtles have senses that we do not yet understand. Some of them **migrate** for thousands of miles across the sea. They return to the exact beach where they hatched. No one knows how sea turtles find their way year after year.

▲ These green turtles are coming to shore on the Galapagos Islands.

migrate   travel in search of food or to breed
survive   stay alive despite difficulties and dangers

Everglades touring

The Everglades are the home of alligators. They live across Florida in swamps, ponds, and drainage canals. They can even appear in marshes along the coast. A few may go into saltwater. In northern Florida, alligators are not active in the cooler winters, but in the south they are on the move all year round. That means they can appear in strange places.

Young alligators stay in the area where they hatched, but then they begin to travel in search of food. If their water holes dry up, they go on the prowl. That is when people sometimes find them in swimming pools or on golf courses.

▼ Crocodiles lurk near the thirteenth hole of a golf course in South Africa.

Incredible journey

Sea snakes can travel a long way. In the 1930s a zoo collector was on a ship in the Pacific Ocean when he saw a strange line in the water. As the boat drew nearer, he saw that it was a solid mass of sea snakes, all moving together. They were orange and black and there were millions. The line of snakes stretched for 60 mi (96 km).

▲ Yellow-bellied sea snakes sometimes get washed up onto beaches.

Reptiles in Danger

Countries with the most pet reptiles (1999)

1. U.S.   7,680,000
2. Russia   4,500,000
3. U.K.   1,730,000
4. France 1,100,000
5. Italy   1,100,000
6. China   612,000
7. Spain   200,000
8. Canada 190,000
9. Thailand 187,000
10. Australia 170,000

Many reptiles are under threat. Their **habitats** are being destroyed or damaged all the time. Another reason why some **species** could become **extinct** is the **exotic** pet trade. More and more people in developed countries want to own unusual reptiles. Wild animals are trapped and sold for high prices. A number of reptiles are at risk.

Perhaps the world's rarest snake is the Antiguan racer. It is a small, **nonvenomous** snake. It was once common on the island of Antigua in the Caribbean. By the 20th century, it had disappeared from the island and was thought to be extinct. Many of the snakes were killed because they scared tourists.

FAST FACTS

Thousands of wild reptiles are caught to supply us with pets. This puts wild snakes and lizards at risk. Many of these pets die because people do not know how to take care of them. Is this the right thing to do?

► An Orinoco crocodile shows its bumpy nose.

Wild Words   **decline**   lose strength or fall in numbers
                                     exotic   from a faraway and unique foreign place

Crocodile in danger

The Orinoco crocodile is South America's largest **predator**. It has a narrow snout and a small bump in front of its eyes. Some males have been reported as being up to 23 ft (7 m) long, but very few above 16 ft (5 m) have been seen lately. The Orinoco crocodile was hunted for its skin from the 1930s to the 1960s. It nearly became extinct and has not recovered since.

Today, there may be only 250 to 1,500 left in the wild. People still hunt them for their meat and eggs, even though it is illegal. Their teeth are also used in traditional medicine. This crocodile is just one of more than twenty reptile species that may not **survive** the next few years.

Turtles under threat

- People eat the eggs of the painted terrapin in huge numbers in many parts of Asia.

- The western swamp turtle is the most **endangered** Australian reptile. The swamps of this turtle's habitat have been drained for farming.

▼ The painted terrapin is one of the most endangered river turtles in Southeast Asia.

extinct   died out, never to return

49

Bad press

Reptiles and us

Reptiles have a hard time. They are not always the cuddliest of animals. Snakes and crocodiles can scare people to the point of panic. Other reptiles bite and do not seem friendly. Because of this, they have been killed in the millions.

Apart from their meat, eggs, and teeth, reptiles have also been hunted for their skins and shells. The demand for snakeskin bags or crocodile-skin shoes and clothes has helped to wipe out vast numbers. This has had a serious **impact** on many natural **habitats.**

It is not all bad news. Many projects to protect and breed reptiles are under way. The Australian pygmy blue-tongued skink had not been seen for 33 years. Then it turned up in 1992. Now its numbers are growing once more.

ALLIGATOR DROWNS BOY

Tavares, Florida   June 19, 2003

A 10-ft (3-m) alligator killed a 12-year-old boy who was swimming near a marina in Florida. He was pulled under the dark water minutes after two friends spotted alligators and screamed for him to get out of the Dead River. "We saw gators all day," said the boy's 14-year-old friend. "Every time we saw them, we would get out of the water."

▶ A loggerhead turtle is being returned to the sea after having its **parasites** removed.

conflict   fight or struggle
crisis   time of danger or turning point

Reptiles matter

Much of the planet is in **conflict.** There have never been more people in the world. We all need space, food, and **resources.** This puts many areas under strain. Building roads and homes beside lakes, rivers, and seas where turtles come to lay their eggs can disturb their nesting. They stop laying eggs, and fewer young **survive.** Garbage in the oceans, such as fishing nets and plastic bags, kills sea turtles and other wildlife. Our **pollution** poisons their world.

Perhaps some of the facts in this book remind us that reptiles are important animals. They have been on Earth for hundreds of millions of years. Reptiles play a vital part of life on this planet. We need to keep it that way.

▲ These are python skins for sale in Cambodia.

pollution   ruining natural things with dangerous chemicals, fumes, or garbage
resources   supplies of materials

Find Out More

Behler, Deborah A. et al. *Snakes*. Tarrytown, NY: Marshall Cavendish, 2001.

Hickman, Pamela. *Turtle Rescue: Changing the Future for Endangered Wildlife*. Westport, Conn.: Firefly Books, 2004.

Miller, Sarah Swan. *Radical Reptiles*. : Franklin Watts, 2001.

Spilsbury, Louise and Richard. *Classifying Living Things: Reptiles*. Chicago: Heinemann Library, 2002.

Zephyr Press Staff. *Curious Critters of the Natural World: Reptiles and Amphibians*. Chicago: Chicago Review Press, 2004.

Website

Smithsonian Institute National Museum of Natural History Division of Reptiles website
http://www.nmnh.si.edu/vert/reptiles/

World Wide Web

If you want to find out more about reptiles, you can search the Internet using keywords such as these:

- **venomous** snakes
- oldest + tortoise
- "Nile crocodile"

You can also find your own keywords by using headings or words from this book. Use the following search tips to help you find the most useful websites.

Search tips

There are billions of pages on the Internet, so it can be difficult to find exactly what you want to find. For example, if you just type in "water" on a search engine such as Google, you will get a list of 50 million webpages. These search skills will help you find useful websites more quickly:

- Use simple keywords instead of whole sentences.
- Use two to six keywords in a search, putting the most important words first.
- Be precise—only use names of people, places, or things.
- If you want to find words that go together, put quote marks around them.
- Use the advanced section of your search engine.
- Use the "+" sign between keywords to link them.

Where to search

Search engine

A search engine looks through a small proportion of the Web and lists all sites that match the words in the search box. It can give thousands of links, but the best matches are at the top of the list on the first page. Try google.com.

Search directory

A search directory is like a library of websites that have been sorted by a person instead of a computer. You can search by keyword or subject and browse through the different sites like you look through books on a library shelf. A good example is yahooligans.com.

Numbers of incredible creatures

Creatures

- Amphibians
- Mammals
- Reptiles
- Birds
- Fish
- Arachnids
- Mollusks
- Insects

Number of species (approximate)
0, 20,000, 40,000, 60,000, 80,000, 100,000, 120,000, 140,000, 160,000, 180,000, 1,000,000

Glossary

acid liquid that can be strong enough to break down materials

aggressive hostile, angry, and bad-tempered

algae types of simple plant without stems that grow in water or on rocks

ambush attack after hiding and waiting

amphibian cold-blooded animal that lives in water and on land

ancient from a past age long ago

bacteria group of very tiny creatures that can cause disease

bask lie in the warmth of the sun

brackish slightly salty

breed produce offspring

camouflage color or pattern that matches the background

cannibal animal that eats its own kind

captivity held in a cage or tank; the way animals are held in a zoo

carbon dioxide gas that animals breathe out

carnivore meat-eater

carrion dead and rotting flesh

chelonians reptiles with hard shells—for example, turtles and tortoises

climate general weather conditions in an area over a period of time

conflict fight or struggle

crest line along the head, neck, and back of some animals

crisis time of danger or turning point

crocodilian reptiles such as crocodiles, alligators, caimans, and gavials

decline lose strength or fall in numbers

diabetes disease in which sugar is not correctly absorbed into the blood

digest break down food in the body

distress call cry for help

duct channel or tube for carrying fluid

endangered at risk of disappearing forever

environment natural surroundings

evolve develop and change over time

exotic from faraway and unique foreign places

extinct died out, never to return

fatal causing death

fertilize when a sperm joins an egg to form a new individual

food chain order in which one living thing feeds on another

forked tongue long tongue that divides into two at the tip

fossil very old remains of things that once lived, found in mud and rock

gall bladder organ of the body that stores bile and acid to break down food

germ very tiny living thing that causes disease

gills organs that some animals have to breathe underwater

gizzard part of a bird's or reptile's stomach that grinds down food

gland part of the body that makes hormones and other substances

habitat   natural home of an animal or plant

herbivore   animal that only eats plants

hibernate   "close down" the body and rest when it is too cold or dry

hypnotize   put someone into a trance

impact   dramatic effect

inflate   blow up and enlarge

insectivore   insect-eater

mammal   warm-blooded animal that has hair and feeds milk to its young

marine   to do with the sea

mate   when a male and female animal come together to produce young

migrate   travel in search of food or to breed

musk   strong-smelling substance

nocturnal   active at night and not in the day

omnivore   animal that eats both plants and animals

oxygen   one of the gases in air and water that all living things need

parasite   animal or plant that lives in or on another living thing

pollution   ruining natural things with dangerous chemicals, fumes, or garbage

predator   animal that hunts and eats other animals

prehensile   able to grip tightly, like a hand

prey   animal that is killed and eaten by other animals

resources   supplies of materials

reticulated   having a pattern of lines and squares; looking like a net

rodent   small mammal with teeth, such as rats, mice, and squirrels

saliva   juices made in the mouth to help chewing and digestion

scales   small, bony plates that protect the skin—for example, on fish and reptiles

scavenger   animal that feeds off scraps and the food of others

scrub   area of thorny bushes and tufts of grass

scute   one of the tough, bony plates that make a tortoise shell

shed   get rid of or lose

species   type of animal or plant

suffocate   choke or die from being unable to breath

survive   stay alive despite difficulties and dangers

thaw   when ice or snow melts

thrive   grow with strength and live healthily

tissue   soft parts of the body; a collection of cells

toxic   poisonous

trance   in a sleeplike state

valve   part that allows movement in one direction only

venom   poison

venomous   poisonous

vertebrate   animal with a backbone

victim   animal that gets hurt or killed

Index